Gingerbread
for all Seasons

Frederick H. Terry

AuthorHouse™
1663 Liberty Drive
Bloomington, IN 47403
www.authorhouse.com
Phone: 1-800-839-8640

First published by AuthorHouse 11/13/2009

ISBN: 978-1-4490-4476-3 (sc)

Library of Congress Control Number: 2009911503

Printed in the United States of America
Bloomington, Indiana

This book is printed on acid-free paper.

PP/Logan, Iowa, USA
11/09, 307534

Introduction

During a dual career as a hospitality management professor and restaurant entrepreneur, Professor Frederick H. Terry would often venture into the community during the holiday season and provide undecorated gingerbread houses, candy and icing to the underprivileged and needy. The experience provided him with numerous opportunities to observe individuals and families enjoying the unique activity of decorating their very own gingerbread creation, usually the only occasion they ever had to do so.

After retiring from teaching, Professor Terry created Gingerbread University ™ in 1998 as a vehicle where families could participate in the joint artistic expression of gingerbread cookie and house decoration, or hold a group or party activity that focused on "good old fashioned family fun."

As an extension of the concept, Professor Terry, an avid storyteller, created stories, usually containing a subtle message, that he could share with the children. As "passive, non-judgmental caricatures who represent no specific race, sect, denomination, or political position," Terry found gingerbread people to be the perfect "imperfect" medium for conveying simple lessons that have universal meaning for all children.

At the urging of the parents of many of his clients, Professor Terry joined with noted artist Anna Fallai and "committed his first story to paper" in 2009. The results, <u>Gingerbread for all Seasons</u>, addresses the universal theme of feeling overlooked and unneeded. With its brilliant, Old European-Style artwork, it is destined to become a classic that will warm the hearts of young and old readers alike.

To all the "little people" of the world who seek
nothing more than to be recognized, loved, and
nurtured and the big people who may still be
searching for these simple gifts.

Once upon a time, in a small village located deep in the mountains, there lived a baker who made fresh breads, cakes, and cookies. Every holiday season, he baked wonderful gingerbread boys and girls whose sweet, spicy aroma filled the air. It was a very special time of the year filled with joy and happiness.

After the holiday season, No-one paid any attention to gingerbread boys and girls. They just sat on the bakery trays feeling very unneeded and sad. "I'll discard them after I finish my bread deliveries," the baker thought sadly. He shut off the lights and went home for the night.

After the baker left, something very magical happened. The kitchen came alive with the sounds of gingerbread boys and girls.

One gingerbread boy announced "Good Grief!, This is not a happy way to end a wonderful holiday season. Let's go visit the wizard on the mountain. Maybe he can find a way for us to be useful. Follow me!" Off the table jumped the gingerbread boys and girls and through the back door they marched. Even the damaged and broken people were carried on a tray! No-one was left behind!

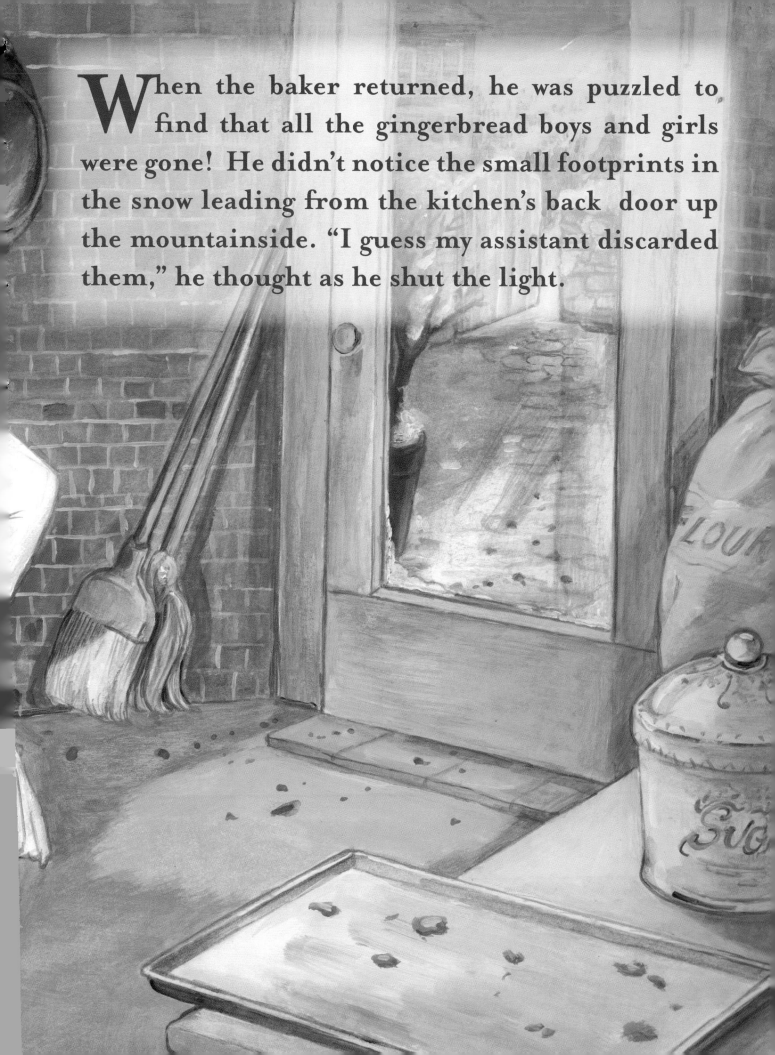

When the baker returned, he was puzzled to find that all the gingerbread boys and girls were gone! He didn't notice the small footprints in the snow leading from the kitchen's back door up the mountainside. "I guess my assistant discarded them," he thought as he shut the light.

The gingerbread boys and girls climbed the mountain until they came to two signs. One had an arrow pointed to "The Valley of the Leprechauns." The other was marked "Wizard." They followed the sign marked "wizard" and soon came to a colorful little cottage high on the mountain. It looked like a gingerbread house. "This must be where the wizard lives," said one Gingerbread Boy.

After knocking carefully on the door, a kind looking man appeared. He was wearing a long blue robe and a pointed hat with stars on it. His bright blue eyes twinkled as he listened carefully to the gingerbread boy's story. "The baker was going to discard us," the boy explained to the wizard. "Even if we're not all perfect, we can be useful and make people happy," a gingerbread girl spoke up. The wizard smiled thoughtfully and began to devise a plan.

The wizard walked with them into the forest to a place he called his *Sharing Circle*. He sat among beautiful pine trees on one of several tree stumps carved with figures of the forest animals. As he shared his plan, the gingerbread boys and girls became very quiet and listened carefully.

Soon after, as the baker was passing Miss McCann's Gift Shop, he noticed her window was full of gingerbread boys and girls decorated with red bows and candy hearts. They held signs stating "I Love You" and "Happy Valentines Day." They looked a little familiar.

"Valentines Gingerbread, What a wonderful idea," he thought, and continued his deliveries.

A short time later, the baker found Miss McCann's window full of gingerbread boys and girls decorated with green candy hats, clover-shaped buttons. and little green shoes. They looked like little elves. "St Patrick's Day Gingerbread, what a wonderful idea," thought the baker, They looked similar to the Gingerbread People he baked during the holidays, but not exactly the same.

Off the baker went on his deliveries.

Spring came and Miss McCann's window was full of gingerbread boys and girls, decorated in beautiful pastel colors. Some of the gingerbread girls even had on bonnets! "What beautifully decorated gingerbread boys and girls," thought the baker. They looked similar to the boys and girls he baked during the holidays, but not exactly the same. He continued on his way.

Next came the special Memorial Day Holiday which honored people who had served their country. Miss McCann's window was full of gingerbread boys and girls with red, white, and blue icing. One was decorated as an astronaut. One was even in a wheelchair! The baker entered the shop and congratulated Miss McCann on her wonderful ideas for decorating gingerbread boys and girls .

"Oh, It's not my idea," exclaimed Miss McCann. "The old man who lives on the mountain sent me trays full of gingerbread to decorate for all seasons." The baker now understood where his leftover gingerbread had gone. The wizard had helped transform them! The thought made him very happy.

Soon news of Miss McCann's brightly decorated gingerbread boys and girls reached far and wide. People came from all over the country to purchase them. One lady was even heard to exclaim, "I've just *Got* to have one!" And with that, if you looked real closely, great big smiles appeared on the faces of all the gingerbread boys and girls in the store.

And from that day on, the gingerbread boys and girls never felt unneeded or sad again. They were loved by all and were carried throughout the land filling everyone's hearts with joy and happiness.